CPSIA information can be obtained
at www.ICGtesting.com
Printed in the USA
BVHW010753061221
623322BV00003B/79